Advance Praise for
I'm a New Widow...What Do I Do Now?

Christine Andrew's new book, *I'm a New Widow...What Do I Do Now?* is practical help for all those experiencing grief. As a father who has lost two children to a rare and always terminal disease, I have read much, both biblical and extra-biblical, on the topic of grief. I have not ever read, however, such a practical approach to the day-to-day reality of loss and what happens next. Christine marries together the practical with the spiritual, bringing all glory to God with her words.

—Joseph Allio,
Retired Chief of Police,
Fairfield, CA

I'm a New Widow...What Do I Do Now? is an invaluable resource and heartfelt encouragement for those who have found themselves in the depths of grief from losing their spouse. Christine Andrew beautifully dovetails scripture with practical experience to create a most helpful handbook for walking through the journey of loss. There is hope in the depths of such grief; Christine shares that journey of hope, transparency and practicality with others. Having experienced the loss of two beautiful daughters, I can tell you that *I'm a New Widow...What Do I Do Now?* crosses over and is applicable to any loss. Thank you, Christine. Well done!

—Kathleen Allio

Christine Andrew has given some good insight and advice for those who find themselves suddenly a widow/widower. This little book is full of practical suggestions and encouraging verses that I believe one will find useful and comforting. Although written with new widows in mind, I believe this book can be a welcome and useful tool for those wanting to assist their grieving loved ones and just don't know where to start. It is an easy read that I can imagine going back to repeatedly to gather one's thoughts, seek encouragement from the Lord, and establish daily goals while in the midst of mourning.

—Tammy Fernandez,
Funeral/Memorial Service Coordinator
Community Bible Church of Vallejo, CA

I'm a NEW WIDOW...
What Do I Do Now?

CHRISTINE ANDREW

Copyright © 2022 by Christine Andrew

All rights reserved. No part of this book may be used or reproduced by any means, graphic, electronic or mechanical, including photocopying, recording, taping or by any information storage retrieval system, without the written permission of the author, except in the case of brief quotations embodied in reviews.

Paperback ISBN 978-1-945169-91-5
eBook ISBN 978-1-945169-92-2

Published by
Mercy & Moxie
An Imprint of
Orison Publishers, Inc.
PO Box 188, Grantham, PA 17027
www.OrisonPublishers.com

Unless otherwise identified, Scripture quotations are taken from the New King James Version®. Copyright © 1982 by Thomas Nelson. Used by permission. All rights reserved.

Scripture quotations marked (KJV) are taken from the King James Version of the Bible. Public domain.

Scripture quotations marked (NIV) are taken from The Holy Bible, New International Version® NIV® Copyright © 1973, 1978, 1984, 2011 by Biblica, Inc.TM Used by permission. All rights reserved worldwide.

Disclaimer:
The information and recommendations outlined in this book are not intended as a substitute for personalized medical advice. Such information in this presentation should not be construed as a claim or representation that any product mentioned constitutes a specific cure, palliative or ameliorative.

Cover photo of Pine Mountain Trail, Cartersville, Georgia, by Christine Andrew

DEDICATION

This book is dedicated to all my friends and family—especially my sisters Linda Hogg-Wood and Kathrine Page; my sister-in-law Jonessa Brittan; my nieces and nephews; and my brothers-in-law—who supported me during the worst time of my life.

I also dedicate this book to new widows (and widowers) who will be experiencing the completion of their marriage vows.

Thank you to the many friends and family who were there for me, offering encouragement and prayers. Also, thanks go to my pastor, Jon Kile, who encouraged me to start writing down my blessings from God, which was the springboard for this book. My thanks also go to the seasoned widows for their experience and wisdom, which also contributed to this book. Finally, thank you to those friends who gave their input and advice in making suggestions for this book and to the entire team at Orison Publishers for their hard work at bringing this book to life cover to cover.

Contents

Chapter One: An Introduction 1

Chapter Two: Who to Call and What to Do 5

Chapter Three: Scriptures of Encouragement 11

Chapter Four: Blessings from Above 21

Chapter Five: Tips for Health
                 During the Grieving Process 35

Chapter Six: Lessons Learned 41

Chapter Seven: To the Church, for Those Who Have
                 Not Yet Lost a Spouse 47

Prayer for Salvation 53

Endnotes 55

Chapter One
AN INTRODUCTION

Death is inevitable. The Bible says in Hebrews 9:27, "It is appointed unto men [and women] once to die" (KJV). We expect that sooner or later our time will come. God, who lends us life, determines when that moment of death must come. This is part of His sovereign will. But, when our husband (or wife, or child) dies and death becomes part of our reality, it feels as if the bottom has dropped out and we cry, "What do I do now?" That's what happened to me. And the more I confer with other widows, the more I realize that I am not the only widow who said those words.

I wrote this book not because I am an expert, but because I have been comforted by God through my own personal journey of loss of a spouse, and if my story can be a comfort and a valuable resource to other new widows (and widowers), then I have been obedient to my calling.

It all started in June of 1994 when I met my soon-to-be husband, Alan. All I ever wanted was to be married and have children. Alan and I married on February 11, 1995. I happily recited my wedding vows. I was finally married at age 39! Children were not in God's plan for us, but we had a wonderful life traveling, attending air shows (Alan was a private pilot, an aircraft mechanic and an aviation enthusiast), gathering with family and friends, playing board games, watching movies together and attending church and church functions. Then, on November 8, 2021, my world stopped. My husband had a massive heart attack. Paramedics got a heartbeat, but my husband was without oxygen for about 20 to 25 minutes. He never regained consciousness or breathed on his own. When the doctors and nurses removed life support after his sixth day in ICU, I said goodbye. The realization that my wedding vows were now fulfilled and that death had parted us, about did me in. I felt that I was the only woman in the world who had lost her husband. We were married for 26 years.

When my husband died, I sobbed, "What do I do now?" In the midst of the shock, I didn't think of going online and seeing what practical resources were out there to tell me what to do. Rather, I needed something immediately. The funeral home had a pamphlet about what to do, but I didn't know about the pamphlet until a week or two later when I met with the funeral director. That was too late. My sister suggested, "Start making a list." With the Holy Spirit's guidance, I set out to make my list of who to call and what to do. That list is in the next chapter for you.

Scores of books on death, the stages of grief, and suffering have been written by accomplished authors. I had

An Introduction

read some. But when hit in the face with my husband's death, I felt like a deer in the headlights, and I froze. There are no manuals about death given out at weddings. When I said the vows, "till death us do part" and "so long as we both shall live" at my wedding, those were just words on a page. I never realized the full impact of those words until years later when I laid my husband in the arms of Jesus.

In the first part of our marriage, we had a simple living trust. After my husband had a stroke, we decided it was probably a good idea to update the trust. In September of 2021, we met with our attorney to do so. My husband wrote the last payment check to the attorney on November 6, 2021. He had the fateful heart attack on November 8. Having a living trust in place is first on the list of what to do.

As a new widow (or widower), you are flying with "unchartered flight plans." It is my prayer that this book will help you with what you need to do and what you need to know, as well as offer resources, encouragement and lessons learned from my own experience. I believe that God allows suffering to come so that we may be able to comfort others who are suffering. I pray that this book will provide you with hope and act as a light to guide you through the darkness.

Johann Sebastian Bach, the famous composer, lost his first wife and three of their seven children. He remarried and then lost his second wife and seven of their 13 children. At the end of his compositions, he wrote the letters SDG for *Soli Deo Gloria*, or "Glory to God Alone." I was soon to understand and express this same sentiment in the months after Alan's passing.

I'M A NEW WIDOW

John 21:19a says, "This He spoke, signifying by what death he would glorify God." God had chosen for Alan (as He does for all of us) what kind of death with which he was to glorify God. God used the heart attack as the door by which Alan would enter his heavenly home. I, on the other hand, was about to walk through another doorway that God specifically designed for me and for all new widows (and widowers) to enter.

Chapter Two
WHO TO CALL AND WHAT TO DO

When my husband unexpectedly passed, I had no manual to guide me in what to do. Instead, I made a list. With the Holy Spirit's guidance, this list became very helpful to me those few days after (and in the months following) my husband's death. As these tasks were accomplished, I tearfully checked them off. My list, included here, is neither exhaustive nor in any particular order. There may be things in it that are not applicable to you; there may be things that are applicable to you that are not on the list. This list is just a starting point for you. Some of these organizations will require a copy of the death certificate.

Who to Call
In the first few weeks, call:
- Trust attorney, to fill out forms and change beneficiaries.

- Doctors and medical insurance companies, to notify of death and cancel any upcoming appointments.
- Pension plan holder, to notify and set appointment to receive husband's pension.
- Social Security (ssa.gov), to arrange for survivor benefits.
- Funeral home, to discuss arrangements.

In the first two months, call:
- Tax accountant, to make the necessary adjustments.
- Financial advisor, to fill out forms, change beneficiaries and send information to the attorney.
- Insurance company for auto, home and life insurance, to notify or cancel spouse's part.
- Department of Motor Vehicles, to change registration.
- Bank, to remove spouse from account.

In time, when you are ready, call:
- Estate sale/garage sale expert, to help in removal of belongings.
- Building inspector, to help in cleanup. (I personally needed this one, as I found out my attic was infested with mice during the prepping for the garage sale.)

Of the organizations on this list, the following will need original death certificate copies sent to them (it can take about four weeks for you to receive these copies):
- Bank
- Tax board

Who to Call and What to Do

- Insurance companies
- Attorney
- Pension or retirement system
- Realtor
- Social Security Administration
- Financial advisor
- Veterans Benefits Administration

What to Do:
In the first few weeks:

(If you are reading this book beforehand and your spouse is still in the hospital or ICU, make sure the hospital has a copy of Durable Power of Attorney and Advanced Health Care Directive. At the same time, set up an online Caringbridge.com account so that friends and out-of-town family can quickly and easily see updates.)

- Pull out trust documents and will; Social Security card for spouse; and marriage certificate and birth certificates, to have on hand.
- Find military discharge papers (DD-214), if your spouse is military.
- Contact Veterans Affairs cemetery.
- Assign someone to make calls.
- Make a list of all family and friends to contact, and contact them through texting, emailing, messaging, etc. An online Caringbridge.com account can also be used.
- Pray. Pray each day for courage and strength to endure the hardship of this new journey that you face.

I'M A NEW WIDOW

- Obtain thank-you cards; keep a list of who has brought things and helped you.
- Assign someone to write thank-you cards.
- Contact the church for a memorial service date and time.
- Plan for the memorial service and burial.
- Assign who is to coordinate bringing food, cleaning up, setting up flowers, arranging photos and memorabilia, attending the guest book, etc., at the memorial service.
- Find photos for the memorial service program and/or slideshow.
- Create the slideshow for the memorial service or assign someone to do so.
- Coordinate or assign someone to coordinate food for the days before the service and for the reception afterward.
- Assign someone to stay at the house during the service.
- Work on an obituary. (Printing an obituary can be expensive. Keep it simple with just basic information. You can find samples online with your town newspaper.)
- Contact a floral shop and plan for disposition of the flowers after the service.
- Remember to get your mail if it is not delivered directly to your house. (Two weeks passed before I realized I needed to collect the mail. This was something my husband always did.)
- Have funds available for unexpected costs. Some of the expenses you may encounter include (in

addition to cremation or burial), flowers, headstone, postage for thank-you notes, attorney fees, obituary printing fees and unexpected house repairs. (I had to change all the locks on the house because I couldn't find my husband's set of keys. I also had to purchase a new set of eyeglasses because I lost mine in all the commotion of settling affairs and preparing for the garage sale. I subsequently found the glasses six months later under the sofa!)

In the first two months:
- Revise homeowners and auto insurance.
- Change the withholding on taxes from married to single. (You should check with your accountant.)
- Cancel spouse's memberships to stores, etc.
- After meeting with an attorney, send a new copy of your Certificate of Trust to your financial advisor and bank.
- Obtain a letter stating the value of your house and the value of your financial assets (IRA, etc.) on the date of death and give it to your attorney.
- Send medical claims to the appropriate insurance carriers.
- Change all billing to survivor's name.

In time, when you are ready:
- Go through old files and shred unnecessary papers with the spouse's Social Security number on them. (You can take these papers to any UPS store and pay by the pound to shred the documents.)

I'M A NEW WIDOW

- Check for any additional benefits, assets or obligations.
- Update your will and trust.
- Revise all IRA, 401K and annual distribution checks to reflect surviving spouse only.
- Change marital status on Facebook, medical account and other relevant accounts.
- Contact accounts with survivor benefits. (Be aware that Social Security benefits will be less for the surviving spouse.)
- Cancel subscriptions. (You can assign someone to do this for you.)
- Cancel spouse's credit cards after all payments are made.
- Change the title on your house.
- Cancel spouse's cell phone after three or four months.
- Make provisions for sale of spouse's vehicle.
- Decide what to do with spouse's belongings: sell, give away, donate, etc.
- Arrange for a garage sale.
- When the dust of all the hustle and bustle settles, when friends and family are gone back to their lives, and the silence hits you—make a backup plan for how you will spend those silent evenings by yourself.

Chapter Three
SCRIPTURES OF ENCOURAGEMENT

Scriptures that spoke of comfort during tribulations took on a deeper meaning for me, providing an abiding peace that is unexplainable.

Blessed be the God and Father of our Lord Jesus Christ, the Father of mercies and God of all comfort, who comforts us in all our tribulation, that we may be able to comfort those who are in any trouble, with the comfort with which we ourselves are comforted by God (2 Corinthians 1:3-4).

During the days and weeks prior to and following Alan's death, I received countless cards and texts of scriptures from friends to encourage and comfort me. I kept a running account of all those scriptures. As the tears came during a sorrowful day, I would return to these scriptures as comfort. The following passages are all the scriptures that I saved, that you can now meditate on and be comforted as I was comforted.

I'M A NEW WIDOW

Numbers 6:24-26
The Lord bless you and keep you; the Lord make His face shine upon you, and be gracious to you; the Lord lift up His countenance upon you, and give you peace.

Psalm 16:8
I have set the Lord always before me; because He is at my right hand I shall not be moved.

Psalm 23
The Lord is my shepherd; I shall not want. He makes me to lie down in green pastures; He leads me beside the still waters. He restores my soul; He leads me in the paths of righteousness for His name's sake. Yea, though I walk through the valley of the shadow of death, I will fear no evil; for You are with me; Your rod and Your staff, they comfort me. You prepare a table before me in the presence of my enemies; You anoint my head with oil; my cup runs over. Surely goodness and mercy shall follow me all the days of my life; and I will dwell in the house of the Lord forever.

Psalm 29:11
The Lord will give strength to His people; the Lord will bless His people with peace.

Psalm 31:24
Be of good courage, and He shall strengthen your heart, all you who hope in the Lord.

Psalm 32:7-8
You are my hiding place; You shall preserve me from

trouble; You shall surround me with songs of deliverance. Selah. I will instruct you and teach you in the way you should go; I will guide you with My eye.

Psalm 34:18
The Lord is near to those who have a broken heart, and saves such as have a contrite spirit.

Psalm 42:5, 8, 11
Why are you cast down, O my soul? And why are you disquieted within me? Hope in God, for I shall yet praise Him for the help of His countenance.… The Lord will command His lovingkindness in the daytime, and in the night His song shall be with me—a prayer to the God of my life.… Why are you cast down, O my soul? And why are you disquieted within me? Hope in God; for I shall yet praise Him, the help of my countenance and my God.

Psalm 46:1, 5, 10a
God is our refuge and strength, a very present help in trouble.… God is in the midst of her, she shall not be moved; God shall help her, just at the break of dawn.… Be still, and know that I am God.

Psalm 54:4
Behold, God is my helper; the Lord is with those who uphold my life.

Psalm 56:3 (NIV)
When I am afraid, I put my trust in you.

I'M A NEW WIDOW

Psalm 61:1-2
Hear my cry, O God; attend to my prayer. From the end of the earth I will cry to You, when my heart is overwhelmed; lead me to the rock that is higher than I.

Psalm 62:2
He only is my rock and my salvation; He is my defense; I shall not be greatly moved.

Psalm 63:1 (NIV)
You, God, are my God, earnestly I seek you; I thirst for you, my whole being longs for you, in a dry and parched land where there is no water.

Psalm 94:19
In the multitude of my anxieties within me, Your comforts delight my soul.

Psalm 116:15
Precious in the sight of the Lord is the death of His saints.

Psalm 121:1-3
I will lift up my eyes to the hills—from whence comes my help? My help comes from the Lord, who made heaven and earth. He will not allow your foot to be moved; He who keeps you will not slumber.

Psalm 143:8
Cause me to hear Your lovingkindness in the morning,

Scriptures of Encouragement

for in You do I trust; cause me to know the way in which I should walk, for I lift up my soul to You.

Psalm 145:21
My mouth shall speak the praise of the Lord, and all flesh shall bless His holy name forever and ever.

Proverbs 3:5-6
Trust in the Lord with all your heart, and lean not on your own understanding; in all your ways acknowledge Him, and He shall direct your paths.

Ecclesiastes 3:1-2, 11a
To everything there is a season, a time for every purpose under heaven: a time to be born, and a time to die; a time to plant, and a time to pluck what is planted;... He has made everything beautiful in its time.

Isaiah 26:3
You will keep him in perfect peace, whose mind is stayed on You, because he trusts in You.

Isaiah 41:10
Fear not, for I am with you; be not dismayed, for I am your God. I will strengthen you, yes, I will help you, I will uphold you with My righteous right hand.

Isaiah 53:3a
He is despised and rejected by men, a Man of sorrows and acquainted with grief.

I'M A NEW WIDOW

Isaiah 54:5
For your Maker is your husband, the Lord of hosts is His name; and your Redeemer is the Holy One of Israel; He is called the God of the whole earth.

Isaiah 55:8-9
"For My thoughts are not your thoughts, nor are your ways My ways," says the Lord. "For as the heavens are higher than the earth, so are My ways higher than your ways, and My thoughts than your thoughts."

Isaiah 58:11
The Lord will guide you continually, and satisfy your soul in drought, and strengthen your bones; you shall be like a watered garden, and like a spring of water, whose waters do not fail.

Daniel 4:34-35
And at the end of the time I, Nebuchadnezzar, lifted my eyes to heaven, and my understanding returned to me; and I blessed the Most High and praised and honored Him who lives forever: for His dominion is an everlasting dominion, and His kingdom is from generation to generation. All the inhabitants of the earth are reputed as nothing; He does according to His will in the army of heaven and among the inhabitants of the earth. No one can restrain His hand or say to Him, "What have You done?"

Zephaniah 3:17
The Lord your God in your midst, the Mighty One, will save; He will rejoice over you with gladness, He will

quiet you with His love, He will rejoice over you with singing.

John 11:25-26a
Jesus said to her, "I am the resurrection and the life. He who believes in Me, though he may die, he shall live. And whoever lives and believes in Me shall never die."

John 14:1-4
Let not your heart be troubled; you believe in God, believe also in Me. In My Father's house are many mansions; if it were not so, I would have told you. I go to prepare a place for you. And if I go and prepare a place for you, I will come again and receive you to Myself; that where I am, there you may be also. And where I go you know, and the way you know.

Romans 8:18
For I consider that the sufferings of this present time are not worthy to be compared with the glory which shall be revealed in us.

Romans 8:28
And we know that all things work together for good to those who love God, to those who are the called according to His purpose.

2 Corinthians 1:3-5
Blessed be the God and Father of our Lord Jesus Christ, the Father of mercies and God of all comfort, who comforts us in all our tribulation, that we may be able to

comfort those who are in any trouble, with the comfort with which we ourselves are comforted by God. For as the sufferings of Christ abound in us, so our consolation also abounds through Christ.

2 Corinthians 4:15
For all things are for your sakes, that grace, having spread through the many, may cause thanksgiving to abound to the glory of God.

2 Corinthians 4:17-18
For our light affliction, which is but for a moment, is working for us a far more exceeding and eternal weight of glory, while we do not look at the things which are seen, but at the things which are not seen. For the things which are seen are temporary, but the things which are not seen are eternal.

Ephesians 3:20
Now to Him who is able to do exceedingly abundantly above all that we ask or think, according to the power that works in us.

Philippians 4:7
And the peace of God, which surpasses all understanding, will guard your hearts and minds through Christ Jesus.

1 Thessalonians 4:13-14
But I do not want you to be ignorant, brethren, concerning those who have fallen asleep, lest you sorrow

as others who have no hope. For if we believe that Jesus died and rose again, even so God will bring with Him those who sleep in Jesus.

2 Thessalonians 3:16
Now may the Lord of peace Himself give you peace always in every way. The Lord be with you all.

Chapter Four
BLESSINGS FROM ABOVE

When we lose our loved one, we encounter many more losses.

The loss of identity. ("Now that I'm single, my social life will change.")

The loss of companionship. ("I don't have anyone to share my deep thoughts with.")

The loss of safety. ("What if I fall?")

The loss of unfulfilled dreams. ("Now we aren't going to go on that vacation we planned.")

The loss of security. ("What if someone breaks in?" "How am I going to manage financially?")

The loss of faith. ("God, why?")

The loss of appetite. (Personally, I didn't eat right or at all for several days.)

The loss of purpose. (Many who lose a spouse are bluntly aware that they are feeling an acute separation phase in their life.)

The list could go on. But, God is more interested that we get through the loss and learn to focus on Him and not on the losses.

Shortly after Alan's passing, someone told me to look for the blessings the Lord was sending my way and to be grateful for those blessings. My pastor encouraged me to write them down. As I pondered what blessings I could find, one event after another came my way. So, I include here the blessings that God chose to bring my way to encourage you. Even the smallest thing could be a blessing granted to you in the midst of sorrow.

Blessings
1) On November 8, the day Alan had his heart attack, a friend from church came right over and sat with me at my house and talked with me while the paramedics tended to my husband. She wanted to pray with me and make sure that I was okay to drive to the hospital. It was a blessing that she was available, and she was very calming for me. She also sat beside me the first Sunday that I went back to church, to make sure that I was not alone.
2) I didn't know what to do immediately afterward. My sister said, "Make a list." As the Holy Spirit moved me, I added items, and that list got longer and longer. When I finally met with the funeral director a week later, she gave me a packet with a list of what to do. Most of those items were already on my list!
3) Alan's death was quick—it was not drawn out as in cancer or dementia.

Blessings from Above

4) I was home when it happened. God, mercifully, had me out of the room when it happened so that I didn't see him have the heart attack.
5) My sister and a close friend came to be with me in the emergency room waiting area. Both were very strong emotionally for me and a great comfort.
6) The ER cardiologist was a Christian and was praying for me and Alan.
7) My chaplain friend from a neighboring town spent two to three hours with me in the hospital lobby, ministering to me while Alan was in ICU.
8) I had the opportunity to share Jesus with ICU nurses and discovered that Alan's last shift nurse was a Christian.
9) In the middle of the Covid era, I got to be in the hospital twice a day, every day. Many families could not be with their loved ones upon death or hospitalization.
10) My twin sister and her husband came to be with me for a week after Alan's death. They both were a huge blessing in helping me get things done, including burying one of my cats that died five days after Alan passed.
11) Lindy (aka Lindbergh, Alan's favored cat of two that we had), our sweet little boy kitty, witnessed Alan's heart attack. The trauma seriously taxed him and triggered his kidney failure. God kept Hannah (Lindy's sister) alive, and she brought me much comfort over the following months. Hannah was a "daddy's girl" and only cuddled with Alan. A few days after he and Lindy passed, Hannah crawled

under the covers with me in bed, laid her head on my ribs and put one paw on my shoulder for quite a long time. Ever since then, she has crawled under the covers after I get into bed and spends about five minutes kneading my abdomen every night. It is such a sweet blessing.

12) At first I fretted about the memorial service reception and where and how to get food and tables set up. The pastor's wife stepped in and said she would take care of everything. I was so blessed when I saw all the food set up and tables prepped at the reception.

13) Many friends came to visit me during Alan's time in the ICU or shortly after his passing, ministering to me and praying with me.

14) The week after Alan passed, my friend Ericka texted me, asking, "What can we do to bless you today?" She and her husband, Mike, and their son came over and helped me organize the boxes in the garage and in the house. They spent about four hours with me. The very next Saturday, Mike collapsed and died. Ericka told me she didn't know what to do. I was blessed to have that list here in this book ready to give her.

15) God has used Alan's and Mike's deaths to draw Ericka and me into a closer bond, which is another sweet blessing.

16) Bobby was in Alan's Bible study group. The two had bonded during the months of being in the group. I had known his wife for many years. Bobby went home to be with the Lord in January. He is buried

about eight rows behind Alan in the cemetery. God used these two deaths to bring his wife and me closer in another special bond.

17) God showered His blessings on me with many cards and texts of scriptures that brought great comfort and encouragement to me.

18) Two weeks after Alan passed, I was in Sonoma visiting my close friend. I backed out of a parking space and scraped the side of my car and another car at the bumper. My taillight was broken. I left my name and number with the other car. A few days later, the owner called me. I told her my husband had just passed away and that I could not deal with this issue, and I asked if she could please wait a couple months. She agreed. That was the first blessing! In January I called her back to ask what she wanted to do now about the repair. She said the car was taken care of and there was no need to pursue anything. That was the second blessing! I then proceeded to look into getting my car repaired because I knew that was what Alan would want me to do. I took it to a local auto body shop to get an estimate. It would cost about $900 to $1,000 to replace the light and repair the scratch. I chose to just replace the taillight. The worker said, "I'll tell you what, if you go to the dealership and purchase the taillight, I will install it for $40." The third blessing! I purchased the taillight for $250 (money that I had already accrued in the auto repair cash envelope—a fourth blessing!) and took it back to the auto body shop. The mechanic fixed it in about 15 minutes.

I'M A NEW WIDOW

The clerk told me, "No charge," as I handed him the $40. That was the fifth blessing!

19) Not too long after the taillight repair, I needed to get my car washed. Since I was watching my spending, I only purchased a ten-dollar basic wash. I sat behind a brand-new BMW. The worker stopped everyone and motioned us all to back up. I did, and the BMW was guided back into the detail section. I was motioned to come forward and go through the wash. As soon as I drove through, all the various lights started to flash. I realized this was not a basic wash. I was driving through the BMW's selection, which was probably the works for $30! Another blessing!

20) Sometime in December I had a dream of Alan. He was standing in the doorway of our bedroom. I could clearly and distinctly tell that it was Alan; it was as if I was seeing him in real life standing there in his favorite clothes. He was smiling and holding a baby. I have not had a dream with him in it since.

21) Sometime in October of 2021, about a month before the heart attack, Alan and I were finalizing our trust. I had asked him to choose whether he wanted to be cremated or buried. He turned to me and responded, "I don't know. Surprise me!" At that time I hadn't thought of what I could do to surprise him. After he died, it came to me! Since he'd had his pilot license for 50-plus years, I wanted to honor him with a surprise (although he will never know this) by sending his ashes up in an airplane for one final flight. I needed

Blessings from Above

a pilot, so I called on his friends at the local airport. The flight plan was then put into place, and we flew over the town for a short spin with Alan's ashes in tow. What a blessing it was for the pilot to offer his services to honor Alan.

22) Being a pilot and an aviation and World War II enthusiast, Alan owned two bomber jackets. One of these jackets went to my oldest nephew. On December 22, after the burial service, my niece gave me a wrapped gift that she had for me from my twin sister who was unable to attend. Before giving the jacket to her son, my sister had rummaged through all the pockets of the jacket. She found something wrapped up in one of the pockets. In the wrapped package were two necklaces. My sister sent the necklaces to me via my niece with a note saying that "apparently Alan had done some early Christmas shopping." However, those necklaces actually came from an Alaskan cruise we had gone on back in June of 2019! Thinking the necklaces were lost, I never thought to rummage through any of his jacket or pants pockets. What a bittersweet blessing and perfect timing to see the necklaces and remember that they came from the Alaskan cruise.

23) Alan and I talked several times about going out to the local VA cemetery, yet we never did. I will never forget driving into the cemetery for the first time on December 22, 2021, for Alan's burial service. The beauty of the cemetery, with its pristine lawns and Christmas wreaths laid at every headstone—it was spectacular and more beautiful than I ever

imagined. And then to see later that Alan's plot was facing the POW/MIA flag and the west mountain slopes that he flew over dozens of times was a most precious blessing. We could not have even planned all that. Only the hand of God accomplished it.

24) In the middle of the following February, I received a notice from one of Alan's former employers that I was entitled to a survivor benefit of Alan's 401(k), even though Alan worked there only for a short time. When I spoke with the financial agent assigned to the 401(k), I found out that the fund was worth several thousand dollars. What a complete blessing that was, as I had no idea Alan had a 401(k)! (This is why it is important to check through everything, including previous employers.)

25) I was privileged to meet and hear stories about Alan from several of Alan's aviation friends whom he frequently and fondly talked about.

26) I sold a bookcase through an online forum to a woman. When I met her to receive her payment prior to the pickup, she asked how I was that day. I was honest and told her, "Not well; my husband just died." She stopped looking at her cell phone and turned to me and said how sorry she was and that she would pray for me. When a couple of guys from church and I delivered the bookcase to her house, she came right up to me, gave me a big bear hug, and told me she was praying for me and would continue to pray. She contacted me several other times through Facebook just to see how I was doing. What a blessing!

27) Alan's good friend Kevin (who teaches pilots how to be pilots) happily took all of Alan's pilot/aircraft mechanic books and paraphernalia to his workplace for the aviation students. That was a huge load off my plate and another blessing! I found out later that his toolboxes went to students at the school. To thank me, the students created a short video of thanks, and Alan's friend sent it to me. It was so special to hear how grateful they were to have acquired all of Alan's tools and toolboxes.

28) I found out from my church that there was a woman who does estate sales. I hired her, and she took over, organizing, setting up, tearing down and donating items to different groups after the garage sale. This was a huge burden lifted from my shoulders.

29) One of my good friends from church just came over unannounced during the week Alan was in the hospital, and even after his death, with pots of soup. She knew what I needed and knew what to bring me on just the right day.

30) My good friend from the local pet shop brought me multiple meals during the week of and the weeks following Alan's death. She also knew what to bring and was always timely as well. She even brought me a "headstone" for Lindy's grave outside in the garden.

31) In November, shortly after Alan's death, I canceled a detox program that I had started him on. It was very expensive, but I had so hoped that it would help turn his health around. I sent a copy of the death certificate to the company, and they refunded my credit card. It wasn't until January when I

got my credit card statement that I saw the credit balance. There were several unexpected expenditures, not budgeted for, that were "paid" for. Now it is March, and I still have a large credit balance. Another bittersweet blessing.

32) As Thanksgiving approached, the thought of being without Alan and alone overwhelmed me, and no one reached out. What a letdown. Even though I didn't really feel like gathering together with people, I felt so alone. Out of that miry clay came a text from a member of the church. He wanted to bring me a pumpkin pie and brought it over a day or so before the holiday. Then my friend and office assistant asked if I had plans for Thanksgiving. Since I didn't, she invited me over. In December another friend invited me over for dinner so that I would not be alone my first Christmas after Alan's passing. These were also enormous blessings.

33) In February 2021, Alan attended a men's conference. He returned with three books. He never purchased books at conferences unless it was an aviation event. One of the books was a couple's Bible study Bible. That told me he was serious about our spiritual growth as a couple. Even though Alan struggled with his speech and comprehension after his stroke, we would take turns reading aloud with the devotional or the scripture. I would ask him, "Do you want to read the scripture or devotion today?" Alan would choose, then I would read the other part. Our marriage grew the greatest during

Blessings from Above

those months, as the passages were springboards to communication and heart-filled discussions. On November 13, the day of pulling life support, I went to Alan's bedside with this couple's Bible study Bible. I opened to the next devotional that we would have read together and told Alan that I was here to do the last couple's Bible study entry with him. I said, "I will read the lesson for the day," and, "Okay, I will lead in prayer today." I read the scriptures and devotional, closed with the prayer, leaned down and kissed him, then said goodbye and told him that I loved him, one last time. Shortly after, Pastor Jon and his wife came for scripture reading, prayer and last song.

After Alan passed, I prayed for several months about who should receive that Bible. I didn't want to toss it or give it to the local secondhand store. The Lord finally revealed to me who the recipient should be. A lady in my Bible study who was fairly new to church, whom I had known for quite a few years, was struggling greatly in her marriage. God clearly nudged me to pass the Bible on to her. I told her the whole story of how that particular Bible came to be. That was truly a blessing as I sat there and witnessed her reaction. I knew I had made the right choice.

34) With Alan's death, my priorities immediately changed. I knew what was important in life—life with Christ and having a trust in place. The legal trust just made everything go easier. I couldn't authorize the removal of life support without the

Durable Power of Attorney or Advanced Health Care Directive. I was so thankful that the trust was literally "hot off the press."

35) God arranged for me to be at my Pilates class so that I would meet a woman whose husband and son-in-law were involved in aviation. So, at the time of opening Alan's toolbox in March, the woman's son-in-law was with me. After looking through the toolbox, we were talking and I found out that he was the son of our friends from another church we used to attend. Alan would have been thrilled to know their son and to know that he was there with me as the final chapter closed and I handed the toolbox over to the airplane hangar owner.

36) Several friends sent me encouraging books to read on suffering and death of loved ones.

37) I am meeting with other widows, and we are encouraging one another. I have a home that I can open up for a Widow's Fellowship meeting.

38) On April 19, I was finishing up packing for a short trip to Kansas to meet my sisters. I figured I would need some cash to take with me on the trip, so I would have to make time to go to the bank. As I was cleaning up the house in preparation for the cat sitter to come, I swooped up some loose change to put in the Amish box that I use for petty cash. I opened the box, and there lay some $20 bills. I counted them up, and it was $200! Oh my gosh; I didn't have to go to the bank. That was the money that came from the extra coins saved up from Alan's coin jar, which

my sister had rolled up back in November and exchanged for bills. I had forgotten about that! Another sweet, timely blessing!

39) On April 21, my sisters and I made our way to Emporia, Kansas, to bury my mom's ashes. Afterward we visited our grandparents' property south of town—a place rich with childhood memories. We greeted the woman who was the current owner, and in just a few moments after meeting her, I found out that she was a widow of only nine months. I told her I was only five months a widow. We both immediately felt a bond, and she told me she had something to give me. She handed me some poems and hymn verses that had kept her going through the recent months. As we parted, she said she would be praying for me. What a gift. This was the woman who occupied my grandparents' home, and we now had a common bond.

40) Perhaps the biggest blessing of all happened the day before Alan had his fateful heart attack. We were standing in the kitchen talking. I don't remember the conversation, but when we were finished, I turned to go do something, and Alan grabbed me and swung me back to him and wrapped his arms around me. He gave me the tightest bear hug ever. I remember just clinging to him and embracing the moment. The next day was his heart attack.

Do I deserve all these blessings? None of us does. Blessings come as reminders that God loves us so much, desires to bless us, and never leaves us nor forsakes us.

I'M A NEW WIDOW

He was constantly my guide and comforter. Continually look for the blessings that come your way, especially in times of sorrow. Just as I was encouraged to write these blessings down, so now I encourage you to write down your blessings as they come your way.

Chapter Five
TIPS FOR HEALTH DURING THE GRIEVING PROCESS

How do we rise to this new life as a widow (or widower)? The following are tips I have learned on this new journey. We continue moment by moment, even through our tears, to choose to do things God's way. Elisabeth Elliot says in her book, *A Path Through Suffering*, "The road you are on is excruciatingly painful, and in many ways will be a means of identifying with Christ in His sufferings"[1] (referring to Colossians 1:24). She was so right. I thought I knew what it was like to suffer loss when my parents died five years prior. Losing a spouse is so exponentially greater a searing pain. The following is a list of ways we can grieve in a healthy way and still bring glory to God.

Recognize the grief. Many books and workshops are available for dealing with grief. New Life Ministries has a "Transforming Grief" workshop available a couple times a year (https://newlife.com/workshops/transforming-grief/).

Cry! And always have your "cry rag" with you. Crying does not mean a crisis until you are somewhere, encounter a trigger, start sobbing and then realize you don't have your cry rag. I learned very quickly how to be creative when that happened to me. Don't feel embarrassed or ashamed when you cry.

Accept the death. Accept yourself as a widow (or widower). Accept God's sovereignty. Accept that at some point you will need to move on. It took me months to accept these truths. The apostle Paul exhorts us in Philippians 3:13, "Brethren, I do not count myself to have apprehended; but one thing I do, forgetting those things which are behind and reaching forward to those things which are ahead." We are not exhorted to forget our loved one, but it is best if we move forward. If we stay stuck, then two lives are lost! What did I do to start moving forward? I redecorated Alan's "man cave" and made it my own. I had a huge garage sale. Every time I visited the gravesite and purchased flowers for the headstone, I purchased a second bouquet for myself. I started a Widows' Fellowship group at my church. I offered to host a "Ladies' Night Out" at my house.

Identify your feelings and offer the grief to God. "If only I had…." "I wished I had…." I said these phrases numerous times during those first few weeks.

Tips for Health During the Grieving Process

Other widows I spoke with said they wished they had more time with their spouses. I have learned, however, that the "if onlys" are counterproductive. Regret can be a prominent feeling after a spouse passes, and it is real. Just don't wallow in these feelings. Romans 12:2 says, "And do not be conformed to this world, but be transformed by the renewing of your mind, that you may prove what *is* that good and acceptable and perfect will of God." I had many regrets. Learn from those regrets and use them to grow. Think about how that regret could have turned out worse and be thankful that it didn't! Regrets can also improve decisions for future use. Gratitude can transform any ill feelings after a loss.

Find a quiet place and pray! Pray and ask God to help you focus on the eternal perspective. I once asked my chaplain friend, Lee, how he gets through so many memorial and burial services without crying. He said that he always focuses on the eternal perspective, not the here and now.

Know that you will be riding waves on this journey. Or, to say it another way, you will be encountering turbulence along this flight. Just don't stay in the turbulence. God wipes away our tears; He doesn't prevent the tears. The turbulences will become calmer.

Focus on the blessings that God can and may bring to you.

Look for new opportunities that come your way.

Nurture yourself. Take relaxing baths, spend time in the sauna, go for a walk, color in a coloring book—take time for activities that relax you.

Recognize that God chose to keep you here to move forward and live out His plan. Thank Him for what He is doing in you through this experience.

Read books. There are many books out there that can help you during this time.

Laugh. Tell funny stories about your loved one. Watch funny movies (our favorite shows were always *America's Funniest Home Videos* and *Monk* reruns).

Get sufficient sleep. Sleep is so important those first few days and beyond. I took extra magnesium threonate at night along with chamomile or lemon balm tea. Melatonin might work for some people as well. (Check with your doctor beforehand. Ask about medication contraindications with these.)

Maintain good nutrition. With the loss of a loved one, a person's resistance to physical illness is often lowered due to the strain on the immune system. The appetite gets lost in all the grief, so it is important to keep up with eating healthy foods during this recovery period. Avoid the sugary desserts and fried foods. Drink plenty of water. In all the planning and grieving, it is easy to forget to drink water.

Exercise is important to maintain, but it can also be a trigger. You will know when you can handle going back to the gym or personal trainer.

The stress of grieving can easily deplete your body of vital minerals such as magnesium. This is one supplement I took that helped me.

Take time off to relax. Read a book, go for a walk, take an Epsom salt bath, do some deep breathing, listen to music (although this was a trigger for me for many months).

Tips for Health During the Grieving Process

Do something fun!

Journal your process or blessings.

Join a support group such as GriefShare, "Transforming Grief" from New Life Ministries, or Widow's Fellowship. A support group can also be just your close friends.

Memorialize (not idolize) your spouse. First Samuel 7:12 recounts how Samuel "took a stone and set it up between Mizpah and Shen, and called its name Ebenezer, saying, 'Thus far the Lord has helped us.'" Build an "Ebenezer" to remember the good things God brought to you to help you through this trying time of sorrow.

Be aware of rejecting others who want to help, or of rejecting yourself.

Be aware of the "letdown." It may happen. People aren't intentionally ignoring you; they may just not know how to approach you.

Lean heavily on grace—grace toward others who don't understand what you are going through. And of course, count on grace from God to get you through each and every day. "My grace is sufficient for you, for My strength is made perfect in weakness" (2 Corinthians 12:9a).

Stay in fellowship with others. Isolation for a time is appropriate to rest, but don't neglect fellowshipping with others. You may still need to set boundaries, though.

Every day be grateful for something. Especially be grateful to our Lord for giving us such a precious gift in our spouse and for blessing the marriage we did share. Job, in Job 1:20, suffered tremendous grief at the loss of his family, but amid that he worshipped God. Also, be grateful for the things you don't like, because God can use that to teach you something or work in you something "more than we could ask or think" (see Ephesians 3:20).

Give yourself time. Contrary to popular opinion, time does *not* heal all wounds, but time does help. Grief has its own timeline, one that is unique to each individual.

Take breaks; get away. You need time to yourself to think, reflect and mourn.

Re-engage in meaningful life, whether it be in work, hospitality or church. Ask the Lord to show you how He can use this time to rediscover meaning in your life.

Wait. People say, "Don't make critical decisions for at least a year." This is good advice. It can be tempting to sell the house, move, take the wedding ring off, etc., but during the grieving process, the brain can't always rationalize properly, and we may end up making a decision we later regret. We are already fighting regrets; we don't want to add to them.

Focus on the love you had with your spouse. First Corinthians 13:13 says, "And now abide faith, hope, love, these three; but the greatest of these is love." Many of us had that verse spoken with our marriage vows. Love will last throughout eternity. In heaven there is no more faith or hope because that will all be fulfilled!

Chapter Six
LESSONS LEARNED

Through reading and gathering with other widows, I gleaned knowledge and understanding and new lessons to help me on my journey. I pass these lessons on to you. When my world came to a screeching halt on November 8, 2021, only two things mattered to me in life. First, where would Alan spend eternity? Second, that we had a trust in place.

I knew without a shadow of a doubt that Alan's eternal home was heaven. He accepted Jesus before we were married. It was some time after his stroke that, when rummaging through some papers, I found a paper that looked like a confession of faith. I asked him if he wrote that, and he said, "Yes!" He didn't date the paper, but I knew then the assurance of salvation for my husband.

Our trust was finalized and in place by November 6. While he was in ICU that week, even as a wife, I could not give permission to remove life support. I had to show proof with the Durable Power of Attorney and the Advanced Health Care Directive. The trust was in place

I'M A NEW WIDOW

and easily accessible to give copies of these documents to the doctors. If you do not have a trust or will in place, get one established for yourself.

Other lessons learned on this journey include the following:

1) God provides and orchestrates everything through ordinary means and natural processes to accomplish His purpose.
2) Heaven is the eternal home of all who love the Lord Jesus Christ. Our Lord is there. All saved family and friends will be there. So those of us who are going there, who believe in Jesus, should receive much comfort and inspiration from our faith in God's promises. The passing of a Christian from this world is not a departure into an unknown world; it is a transition to a place prepared for him or her by the Lord Jesus.

    If you do not have the assurance of heaven as your eternal home, I invite you to accept Jesus Christ as your personal Savior. At the end of this book, I have included a prayer you can pray to invite Jesus into your heart so that you, too, can have assurance of your eternity.
3) Grief is the price we pay for love.
4) Triggers will come. They can come from having a dream, listening to worship music, looking at photos, attending an event such as a wedding, anniversary or other special occasion, seeing the word *deceased* next to your spouse's name on a document, and even from someone asking, "How are you?" …

and the flood of tears wells up. As time passes, the triggers will still be there, but the tears are less.

5) The companionship and intimacy that we enjoyed here on earth with that person is over, never to be recaptured. We must face the truth of that and remember not to cry because it is over (although I did cry greatly because it was over and the marriage contract was completed), but to smile and rejoice because it happened.

6) It would be easy for God to spare a life, but He performs a greater miracle when He changes our life attitude and strengthens our faith and trust in Him. The day that Alan's life support was removed, I was allowed to stay and watch the process. I literally witnessed the miracle of Alan passing from his earthly body into eternity. Our loved ones are not lost. They have only gone home before us. For them the experience is one of gain rather than of loss. They have been freed from their earthly flesh. They are present with the Lord, as 2 Corinthians 5:8 assures us.

7) Philippians 4:11-13 reminds us that God is able to supply us with every resource we need to get through the trial. God's promises never failed me through this or any other trial. He is a faithful God. Psalm 68:5 reminds us that God is not only the Father of the fatherless, but also the protector of widows.

8) Heaven is not here. Earth is just our footstool. In her book *A Path Through Suffering*, Elisabeth Elliot said, "If we were given all that we wanted here

on this earth, our hearts would settle for this world rather than on the next."[1]

9) In other lessons from Elisabeth Elliot in *A Path Through Suffering*: "A well-pruned vine bears the best fruit."[2] She writes, "We surrender ourselves to the Lord, learning day by day to treat all that comes to us with peace of soul and firm conviction that His will governs all."[3] She also writes, "He even provides for us the conditions which may make us fruitful. It's not just for our sake, but for the sake of others."[4]

10) God does not necessarily think we are strong enough to go through this experience, but rather we are strengthened by Him through this trial. Philippians 4:13 says, "I can do all things through Christ who strengthens me."

11) Albert Martin said in *Grieving, Hope and Solace: When a Loved One Dies in Christ*, "Few things more quickly and effectively snap some of the shackles that bind us to this world than does the death of a dearly loved one."[5] He was so right. It felt so freeing to have my garage sale after Alan's death. It was freeing not to be bound by what was the latest on the nightly news anymore.

12) Psalm 90:12 says, "Teach us to number our days, that we may gain a heart of wisdom." How easy it is to forget this truth and forget our vow of "till death us do part." I know I personally gained a greater sense of my own and my family members' mortality. I have a renewed determination to live well in light of this truth.

13) Now that our loved one has passed, our responsibilities as a Christian need to continue. We are no longer a spouse, but there may still be children, parents or grandparents who need to be looked after; a job that needs to be returned to; leadership in a ministry that will need attention. First Timothy 5:4-5 instructs widows to show godliness to their household and to continue in prayers. The duties will need to be adjusted temporarily during our most intense grieving period, but as we grow stronger, the daily or weekly activities can be resumed.
14) Rest in the assurance that wholeness will come to you. Matthew 11:28 says, "Come to me, all you who are weary and burdened, and I will give you rest" (NIV).
15) For me, the death of my spouse provided the richest opportunity to learn the deepest lessons anyone could learn.
16) John MacArthur says in his book, *The Power of Suffering,* "Gentle and tender hearts are the product of great troubles."[6] Perhaps this is what God is producing in me?
17) "Whenever God brings us through a severe trial [like the death of a spouse] it will reveal to us either the strength or weakness of our faith and the faithfulness of God. It will wean us away from worldly things. It calls us to a greater realization of our eternal hope. It makes us long for heaven even more. It shows us what we really love. It teaches us to value the blessings of God. It enables us to help others in their suffering," MacArthur writes.[7]

Chapter Seven
TO THE CHURCH, FOR THOSE WHO HAVE NOT YET LOST A SPOUSE

You may not yet have lost a spouse or a loved one, but here is a list of tips to help you be a comfort to a new widow. (These could also apply to a widower.)

"Rejoice with those who rejoice, and weep with those who weep" (Romans 12:15). It doesn't add, "if you happen to be in a rejoicing or weeping mood." A widow can start crying from any trigger. Be there to both comfort and rejoice. In her book, *Healing After Loss*, Martha Whitmore Hickman quotes a friend who said, "If someone cries in front of me, I consider it a gift."[1]

Connect with the widow. Listen; check in with her with texts, phone calls, cards or in person. Hug her.

I'M A NEW WIDOW

Assist with tasks. Don't wait to be asked. The widow has no idea what she needs help with until she needs help.

Refrain from saying, "Let me know if you need anything." Again, usually, the widow has no idea what she needs. A widow is too overwhelmed and won't remember who said that anyway. Reach out to help by phone call or text and say, "I'm available; how can I bless you today?"

Don't be afraid to talk about her loss and feelings. Allow her to share thoughts. You might even want to ask, "Do you feel like talking now, or would you rather be left alone?"

Never assume the widow is busy with family. She may be alone and feeling lonely even though she knows Jesus is with her.

When you say, "How are you?" be ready to listen to hear how the widow really is doing. Too often people use the phrase "How are you?" synonymously with saying, "Hi" and don't stop to really find out how the widow, or anyone, for that matter, is doing. The very fact that you genuinely ask acknowledges and affirms that you remember and care about the person who has passed. That alone blesses the widow. Life goes on when a person dies, but not to a new widow. She remembers her love every day.

Resist the urge to fix the widow or explain why the death happened. There is a little story I read in Martha Hickman's book, *Healing After Loss*, about a little girl who visited her friend and got home later than expected. Her mother asked the reason for the delay. The child said that she was helping her friend because her friend's doll broke. The mother asked if she had helped her friend fix the doll. The child responded, "No, I helped her cry."[2] That is what widows need.

Sometimes all you need to say is, "I'm sorry."

Refrain from asking a widow, "Are you over it?" A widow may never be over her husband's death.

Resist the urge to say, "He's in a better place." This does not help a grieving widow.

Recognize the "firsts" in the lives of widows—first birthday, anniversary or holiday without their spouses.

As time goes on, check in again. Widows need people to help us, listen to us, hold us and remember our loved one with us. This keeps the loved one's memory alive.

Pray with them.

Plan an activity together, such as a meal, a walk, an event, etc.

A friend in May of 2022, six months after my husband died, sent me a typed copy of the following: "I am a griever. That doesn't mean I have a disease. It means that I miss and love someone who has died. Let me grieve at my own pace. My reality is forever changed. Do not judge me nor feel it is your obligation to tell me to 'move on' or 'get over it.' Getting over it is not an option. With time, I will do my best to move forward one step in front of the other. They might be baby steps, but it is better than none at all. When I need you… Just be there."[3] Everyone grieves differently and in their own way and time, depending on the nature and circumstances of the relationships.

I'M A NEW WIDOW

Have a "flight" plan ready. A pilot never gets on a plane without a flight plan in place. If you do not have a living will or trust in place, get it done. It will make things so much easier and will be more cost effective when that time comes for you. If you don't want to do a trust, then consider a "Five Wishes." It is available online at www.fivewishes.org for five dollars. This is a legal document that you can fill in with your wishes—wishes for who you want to make decisions for you when you can't; the kind of medical treatment you want or don't want; how comfortable you want to be in a hospice or terminal condition; how you want people to treat you; and a personal message of things you want your family and loved ones to know.

Have a separate document prepared with necessary information like your phone number; address; date and place of marriage; people and organizations to notify, such as accountant, physician, clergy, financial advisor, other family, specific friends, business or job contacts, bank, utilities, Realtor, mortuary of preference, and insurance companies; and paperwork such as title, pension and retirement information, medical policies, computer passwords, specific funeral and burial instructions, memorial service instructions, personal property distribution, etc. Fortunately, I had already had this separate document set up, which made it easily accessible to know who and how to notify these organizations and accounts.

Statistically, men die first. It is prudent to first have a trust so that all bills and accounts are in both

To the Church, for Those Who Have Not Yet Lost a Spouse

names. Some accounts such as for store memberships and phone companies have a primary holder. Switch the primary to the wife's name. Even with a trust, it seemed to take almost an act of Congress to switch these accounts to my name.

PRAYER FOR SALVATION

Therefore we do not lose heart. Though outwardly we are wasting away; yet inwardly we are being renewed day by day....what is seen is temporary, but what is unseen is eternal (2 Corinthians 4:16, 18, NIV).

Everyone dies physically at some point, but those who believe in Jesus Christ are promised a physical resurrection for eternal life in heaven. You see, God has made a way for all of us to be forgiven of our sins to give us assurance of life in heaven for eternity. He did that by sending His Son, Jesus Christ, to take the sins of mankind on Himself through dying on a cross. He was buried and then raised on the third day.

If you have not accepted Jesus Christ as your Lord and Savior and if you want assurance of salvation for eternity in heaven, then you, too, by faith, can accept His free gift and forgiveness of sins by praying this prayer that my husband wrote out and prayed:

I'M A NEW WIDOW

"Heavenly Father, I believe You love me just as I am. I confess that I cannot run my life on my own, and I ask You to forgive me for trying. I confess that I have been separated from You and have sinned. I ask You to forgive me. I invite Your Son, Jesus Christ, to come into my life and be my Savior and Lord. By Your grace, I will seek to follow You day by day, moment by moment. If I fall, I will come to You immediately and ask You Your forgiveness and restoration. I cannot live without Your grace. For it's in Your holy name I pray these things, Lord. Amen."

Alan E. Andrew

Soli Deo Gloria

Endnotes

Chapter Five: Tips for Health During the Grieving Process
1. Elisabeth Elliot, *A Path Through Suffering* (Grand Rapids, Michigan: Revell, 2014), 146.

Chapter Six: Lessons Learned
1. Elisabeth Elliot, *A Path Through Suffering* (Grand Rapids, Michigan: Revell, 2014), 188.
2. Ibid., 36.
3. Ibid., 59.
4. Ibid.
5. Albert N. Martin, *Grieving, Hope and Solace: When a Loved One Dies in Christ* (Minneapolis, Minnesota: Cruciform Press, 2011), 95-96.
6. John MacArthur, *The Power of Suffering: Strengthening Your Faith in the Refiner's Fire* (Colorado Springs, Colorado: David C. Cook Publishing, 2011), 147.
7. Ibid., 31.

Chapter Seven: To the Church, for Those Who Have Not Yet Lost a Spouse
1. Martha Hickman, *Healing After Loss: Daily Meditations for Working Through Grief* (New York: William Morrow, 1994), February 5.
2. Ibid., July 21.
3. Missing Loved Ones (www.facebook.com/Missinglovedones, 2014).

To Christine
I left with wintry winds
Upon their sails I rode.
A gentle Hand reached down,
I quickly took a hold.
He led me where no eye has seen,
No ear has ever heard.
A place no mind has imagined
As He said in His word.
My days are sweet, my life complete
All things have been made new.
It's everything He promised,
His love so rich and true.
I watch and wait for that sweet day,
when you will be here too.
But until then know that I'm here in Heaven,
loving you. Love, Alan

Written by Donna Hoover
August 4, 2022

www.ingramcontent.com/pod-product-compliance
Lightning Source LLC
Chambersburg PA
CBHW052123110526
44592CB00013B/1724